HAPPY BIRTHDAY!
LOVE,
Randy, Sue and Randy T.

MADISON SQUARE PRESS
GROSSET & DUNLAP
A NATIONAL GENERAL COMPANY
Publishers   New York

The Illustrated
Leaves
of Grass
by Walt Whitman
Introduction by
William Carlos Williams
Edited by Howard Chapnick

*To Jeanette, Denise and Ilene — the three ladies
in my life who have shared my romance with Walt Whitman.*

Preface

Walt Whitman's poetry is eternal. The nineteenth century poet becomes the twentieth century prophet.

All wars have the common denominator of death. Hear his words of Gettysburg and he could be describing Verdun or Bastogne or Khe Sanh. "In midnight sleep, of many a face of anguish, of the look at first of the mortally wounded—of that indescribable look; Of the dead on their backs, with arms extended wide, I dream, I dream, I dream."

The names of the assassins change, but my "Captain" be he Lincoln or Kennedy, "lies fallen cold and dead."

Whitman's "shapes of democracy" and "shapes of turbulent manly cities" evoke equal visions of conflict and confrontation in the continuous expression of democratic dissent. The elapsed century ties these threads of dissent from the Draft Riots of 1863 to the Chicago Convention of 1963.

Walt Whitman was probably the most visual of American poets. In the 20th century when the visual image has become transcendent, photographic poets have emerged. I have sought a marriage of words and pictures hoping to add new dimension to Whitman's poetry.

It was impossible to use all of Whitman's poetry in this volume, but hopefully this sampling will stimulate readers to further savor the full breadth of his work.

Howard Chapnick

Acknowledgments
To Yukiko Launois and Jill Losson with great appreciation
for their inspired photographic research and assistance.

Contents

Preface 5

Introduction by William Carlos Williams 9

Excerpts from "Song of Myself" 14

Excerpts from "I Sing the Body Electric" 72

"To Old Age" 80

Excerpts from "Song of the Broad-Axe" 88

"Song of the Open Road" 104

Excerpts from "Faces" 116

"Pioneers! O Pioneers!" 126

"Song at Sunset" 132

Excerpts from "When Lilacs Last in the
   Door-yard Bloom'd" 134

"O Captain! My Captain!" 144

"A Carol of Harvest" 146

"Carol of Occupations" 158

Excerpts from "Crossing Brooklyn Ferry" 170

"An Old Man's Thought of School" 172

"There Was a Child Went Forth" 174

"That Music Always Round Me" 182

"In Midnight Sleep" 184

"It Is I Too, the Sleepless Widow" 186

"Good-bye My Fancy!" 188

"I Bequeath Myself to the Dirt" 190

Introduction

A democratic book has a profoundly covert aspect, especially if it be a book of poems. This is true of Walt Whitman's *Leaves of Grass,* and affected the construction of the poem long past the poet's lifetime. There were tenets in his fundamental beliefs that forced on him a more liberal measure than the classic for his verses. Following his native idiom he declared himself a poet, a vein not to be accepted by many of his fellows. It took courage. A fellow countryman, himself a great writer, Herman Melville, completely missed the point. It was the distinctive measure of the age that linked him with the great of the past. Whitman's song, "I Celebrate Myself," was a revolutionary blast whose measure was not appreciated beyond the noise that signalled it to the world that turned askance at it.

It was a revolution in the language he was employing to communicate between man or woman, either way, and that he was intent on accomplishing. If this is not a gift of language, what then is it? It was the gift of the idiom he knew.

He was a man who knew what he meant to say in speaking his mind. He used the words that came handiest to him and he looked no further. He was a Quaker or close to it when he was growing up. Wandering south after a job when he was a young man he is said to have met a young woman not far from New Orleans and made love to her and she to him. But his intimates heard of it and broke it up referring to her dark skin — he never forgot her during his entire life. Those things are not to be put lightly aside by that measure of a man.

Coming north again after he had turned right and left in pursuit of his woman, he was forced finally to give her up. His sorrow became the business of everybody who knew him. Poets had their moving sorrows before; if he could not have this beautiful woman for his own, to hell with it, but no one should know by his confession the depth of his resentment against this humdrum world of his fellow beings. He decided he wanted to be a printer. No doubt at the back of his head he wanted to write as others had done before him; he could learn to write.

The day Whitman began to write, freedom was in the air. You can write without freedom, but if it is mixed with the love of a woman, what happens? A poet's love. This poet's love made him speak out the way he wanted to. That's poetry because I say it is poetry and no one can say it is not poetry.

The American idiom is my language, he said, to write a book called *Leaves of Grass* because leaves of grass can be found everywhere in my country. I'll open my mouth where I happen to be standing and let the world hear what I happen to say because it is also what they of the world have to say — and so we shall be singing together because we are one.

There is an art of poetry, Whitman said. I can't bother about that. It is attested by the witness of many voices, granted. I haven't at the moment time for it.

Students of English from the chairs of many distinguished universities, here and abroad, were arrested by the sheer impudence of the man and saluted him finally as a wild but gifted poet. At the same time they failed to acknowledge his presence as any more than an aberrant species, without knowing that in the end they might very well have to modify their point of view. A jarring note had been struck by Whitman. The use of the language in the New World might have to be modified — if not yet, eventually — to accommodate the more variable principle enunciated for the first time by this man. With a shock we realized that, postpone as we may, this was the time our rigid dictates would be modified.

When Walt turned his back definitely on blank verse, and in the excitement of a poet's mind imagined himself free, he was in the main mistaken; on the other hand, he established himself as the greatest poet we shall ever know. To speak of verse as "free" is a contradiction in terms, an impossibility. Measure is the *sine qua non* of all verse; verse cannot exist without it. When Whitman abandoned blank verse, the iambic pentameter, and turned to the American idiom for release, by the same gesture he turned away from an established custom. He was turning toward the unknown future, knowing that he did not know its profound implications.

The critical attacks from England were to be expected, and to Whitman's credit he took them in stride. They were chiefly notable for their heat rather than any light they cast over the critical situation. As soon as he had established himself, facing the public, the din opposing him was deafening. And, as usual, he was attacked chiefly on moral grounds both here and abroad. Scandal attached to his name, as had been the case with all art through the ages. At least he was not burned at the stake for his poems, no thanks to his readers. What no one at the time detected was that his attack on "The Establishment" would have to be long postponed for its effectiveness — hard as it is even now to realize. The Establishment, all there is virulent in Church and State, was drawn up in this attempt to repel the enemies of law and order stalwart under the attack, really under the attack in vulgar guise of the local idiom.

The whole of what constitutes the English had been questioned.
It is not until the present day, the dawn of a new age, that it has been realized how deep Whitman had disturbed the prosody of past ages by his instinctive release under the primitive conditions in his native country, an idiom which he adopted without question. It is all he knew, and he would not retreat into the past to escape it. Self-willed, it was all or nothing with him. Whitman's attack had to take a chance at being violently mistaken, for it was directed at the first of all verse verities, measure itself, a revaluation of the underlying principles which carried it. That the entire structure might be outmoded occurred to no one else of his generation.

English verse had crystallized about the iamb ever since the race had come into being. Before *Chaucer* and *Beowulf* the pattern had long since been set. The Elizabethans had gripped it into the particular form of their blank verse, the iambic pentameter, until the whole of Christendom would accept nothing else as characteristic. To many, then, Whitman was no better than a heathen. The "Establishment" and all its universities recognized at once that it was threatened. It is strange how universal the "flight to the colors" can be. The conservative French, on the same language tree, who could yield a point without sacrificing anything, retreat to the cover of their *academie,* but they were not so intimately involved, were more flexible in one way, so they could absorb their Paul Fort without undue strain. But the English "got a fright."

There was among the Elizabethans a movement to adopt the hendecasyllabic or 2-syllable line of the classic Greek, but it was not practicable for the language. Admiring songs like those in the poems of Campion, it sometimes aspired to release itself from the iambic pentameter of blank verse. But this latter had no difficulty in maintaining its dominance until a new language began to insinuate itself among the new roots — covertly, at first, against the ridicule that Whitman encountered.

Whitman's blood was singing within his veins .   .   .

I

Out of the cradle endlessly rocking,
Out of the mocking-bird's throat, the musical shuttle,
Out of the Ninth-month midnight,
Over the sterile sands, and the fields beyond, where the child, leaving his bed,
    wander'd alone, bare-headed, barefoot,
Down from the shower'd halo,
Up from the mystic play of shadows, twining and twisting as if they were alive,
Out from the patches of briers and blackberries,
From the memories of the bird that chanted to me,
From your memories, sad brother — from the fitful risings and fallings I heard,
From .under that yellow half-moon, late-risen, and swollen as if with tears,
From those beginning notes of sickness and love, there in the transparent mist,
From the thousand responses of my heart, never to cease,
From the myriad thence-arous'd words,
From the word stronger and more delicious than any,
From such, as now they start, the scene revisiting,
As a flock, twittering, rising, or overhead passing,
Borne hither — ere all eludes me, hurriedly,
A man — yet by these tears a little boy again,
Throwing myself on the sand, confronting the waves,
I, chanter of pains and joys, uniter of here and hereafter,
Taking all hints to use them — but swiftly leaping beyond them,
A reminiscence sing.

II

Once, Paumonok,
When the snows had melted — when the lilac-scent was in the air, and the Fifth-month grass
    was growing,
Up this sea-shore, in some briers,

Here and there and from time to time certain flaws had appeared in the solid masonry of English speech; but nothing to undermine its fundamental basis as Whitman's poetry threatened to do if taken seriously. Here, unsuspiciously, this voice from the New World was little more than that of a wild man, though curiously enough, the nearer they approached the Greek the more sympathetic they became to the new language. Actually, Gerard Manley Hopkins had a sizable correspondence with Whitman. Something had disturbed the sense of balance which these men were maintaining between their day and the present.

Whitman could not satisfy himself with the measure he was asked to dance in such poems as "When Lilacs Last in the Dooryard Bloom'd" and, we'll say, "Compost." Whitman was not misled by his poetic instincts, but he saw no further than the age permitted him. It would have been impossible for him to outstrip the mathematicians, 'tho he trod on their heels as many poets have done in the past to complete the poetic gesture. He was not satisfied with standard British verse the way it was presented to him by the New England poets. In fact, their blank verse nauseated him as it did some of his illustrious British confreres.

The measure was wrong!

His attempt to sing was laughed at as boorish, scandalous, shocking! Ladies cannot tolerate such kitchen cavortings. Such dislocations of the orderly progress of the minuet by the unmannerly hiccupings and gruntings and worse could not be tolerated. The polite trend of events was changing not so much to ruder standards but to accommodate a measurement of a different order. The line was not to be counted as it had been heretofore. The musicians and painters knew this better than the poets. The physicists knew it best of all.

This was to affect the poetic line; Whitman anticipated this. The variable foot is a term that was invented to take care of the present poetic division of the term accompanying "the American idiom." A foot, dactylic or iambic, may be largely ignored in modern prosody, but everyone understands what is meant, as one knows what is meant when a spondee is spoken of. So it must be when a variable foot is spoken of, an unstable foot. In Whitman's verse there are many simple examples of it, but he did not exploit the timing as much as he might have to enhance the variety of his line. This is of supreme importance as the line has developed in modern poetry.

Although The Establishment did not yet acknowledge it, blank verse as sanctified by the dramatists of the Elizabethan age had become a norm which it was dangerous to ignore. The *Iliad* with its pentasyllabic sweep resembled Whitman when his measure faced the sea along the New Jersey shore with the waves beating in. The beat of the ultra-modern line of the present day — when it is recognized as representing anything at all among the ignoramuses — owes much to Whitman for taking his bold stand. All modern American poets must acknowledge that they date, when it comes to the measure of their verses, from Whitman. At the same time it must be acknowledged that the inheritance does not *seem* to be direct. But it is. It comes directly out of the American, his own common speech — and not out of the iambic pentameter. In one of his most important poems, the "Song of Myself," he from the first announces the basic and rebellious principle from which he would never waver — no matter how it may be varied and expanded. That magnificent apostrophe, which to many sounded like the raving of a mad man, we should read still — discounting what we have to — with closest attention. Poets and scholars may well dig into it for their gold.

Whitman came from a rhetorical and long-winded age, but that doesn't offset the basis of what is to be learned from him. That is the measure of the new language of today. The classics are not to be ignored. The essential tautology of the bad writing which many of our present poets can be accused of must still be faced. Brevity and stylistic invention are still virtues.

When I first saw the photographs that were being presented to me I was thrilled. Never to my knowledge had the subjects of Whitman's Leaves of Grass been so presented! The poem came alive for me as if for the first time. It needed just that breadth and depth of vision to get the significance of the smallest minutiae represented in the poem for its understanding, which only the modern in photographic equipment can give.

As photograph after photograph was uncovered for me I realized how much we are losing in the hurry of the movies and their later developments. I have long realized their triviality compared, for instance, with a well-taken still by a master. You can see nothing until the eye has been stopped in its tracks and at last it is permitted to take its own time to penetrate into the depths of the picture — to turn about in the full sense of Whitman's

> I lean and invite my Soul;
> I lean and loaf at my ease, observing a spear of grass.

This the photographs were accomplishing before my eyes. It amounted to a new technique which made the flickering movie obsolete — an impertinence. Don't try to throw the ball before you have caught it, many a ball player has learned to his sorrow. Our screen has still to learn this lesson from such magnificent photographs as these. You cannot rush away from them before you have grasped them, held them to the heart at least for a moment, made them your own. Looking into the depths of an old woman's eyes, the eyes of a Tennessee mountain woman, slightly averted, which you have somewhere seen before; suddenly you realize that they are the eyes of a cartoon you have all of you been familiar with for many years and before which you turn aside in embarrassment covering your shame. Before this grotesque image we have all of us guffawed. Whitman has dignified this poignant figure of our southern states, which shockingly our photographers have placed on the page in all her tragic significance.

We all need to pause before the contemplation of our lives before we can laugh or cry. We are dying for it, literally dying for it. These magnificent stills give us the opportunity to pause and look around as we have wanted to, as in the case of this mountain woman in the depths of whose eyes so much brute suffering lies hid. Look in this photograph and you will see what Whitman saw in her eyes and recorded in his poems — which the photograph picks up for us to dwell upon and study at greater leisure.

Every photograph is a reaffirmation of life's permanence into which you may step to discover new details of flower, submarine vista, or cloud, new details of icy barnyard snowswept under a lowering sky — as Whitman saw it and we in the same track see it today.

It is the art of the photograph which stops us in our tracks almost against our wills, fixes us not to ridicule as in the funnies but to give us back, if we have any of it left, that dignity that Whitman has proclaimed for us as human beings.

WILLIAM CARLOS WILLIAMS

NOTE:
The introduction written by William Carlos Williams dates back to 1960 when this illustrated "Leaves of Grass" was first conceived. Many of the original photographs have been changed — not in context or interpretation — but to reflect the changes in contemporary photography over the past decade.

Excerpts from "Song of Myself"

I celebrate myself;
And what I assume you shall assume;
For every atom belonging to me, as good belongs to you.

I loafe and invite my Soul;
I lean and loafe at my ease, observing a spear of summer grass.

Houses and rooms are full of perfumes — the shelves are crowded with perfumes;
I breathe the fragrance myself, and know it and like it;
The distillation would intoxicate me also, but I shall not let it.

The atmosphere is not a perfume—it has no taste of the distillation—
       it is odorless;
It is for my mouth forever — I am in love with it;
I will go to the bank by the wood, and become undisguised and naked;
I am mad for it to be in contact with me.

The smoke of my own breath;
Echoes, ripples, buzz'd whispers, love-root, silk-thread, crotch and vine;
My respiration and inspiration, the beating of my heart, the passing
       of blood and air through my lungs;
The sniff of green leaves and dry leaves, and of the shore, and
       dark-color'd sea-rocks, and of hay in the barn;
The sound of the belch'd words of my voice, words loos'd to the
       eddies of the wind;

A few light kisses, a few embraces, a reaching around of arms;
The play of shine and shade on the trees as the supple boughs wag;
The delight alone, or in the rush of streets, or along the
        fields and hill-sides;
The feeling of health, the full-noon trill, the song of me
        rising from bed and meeting the sun.

Have you reckon'd a thousand acres much? have you reckon'd the
        earth much?
Have you practis'd so long to learn to read?
Have you felt so proud to get at the meaning of poems?

Stop this day and night with me, and you shall possess the origin of all poems;
You shall possess the good of the earth and sun — (there are millions
        of suns left;)
You shall no longer take things at second or third hand, nor look through
        the eyes of the dead, nor feed on the spectres in books;
You shall not look through my eyes either, nor take things from me:
You shall listen to all sides, and filter them from yourself.

A child said, *What is the grass?* fetching it to me
        with full hands;
How could I answer the child? I do not know what it is,
        any more than he.

I guess it must be the flag of my disposition, out of hopeful
        green stuff woven.

Or I guess it is the handkerchief of the Lord,
A scented gift and remembrancer, designedly dropt,
Bearing the owner's name someway in the corners, that we may
        see and remark, and say, *Whose?*
Or I guess the grass is itself a child, the produced babe of the
        vegetation.

Or I guess it is a uniform hieroglyphic;
And it means, sprouting alike in broad zones and narrow zones,
Growing among black folks as among white;
Kanuck, Tuckahoe, Congressman, Cuff, I give them the same, I
        receive them the same.

And now it seems to me the beautiful uncut hair of graves.

Every kind for itself and its own —
          for me mine, male and female;
For me those that have been boys,
          and that love women;
For me the man that is proud,
          and feels how it stings to be slighted;

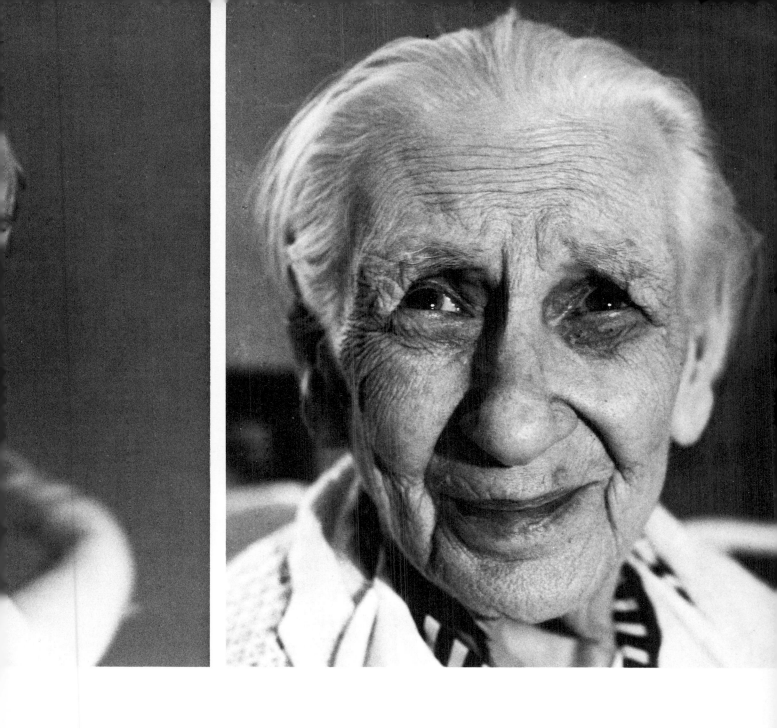

For me the sweet-heart and the old maid —
    for me mothers, and the mothers of mothers;
For me lips that have smiled,
    eyes that have shed tears;
For me children, and the begetters
    of children.

The big doors of the country barn stand open
       and ready;
The dried grass of the harvest-time loads
       the slow-drawn wagon;
The clear light plays on the brown gray
       and green intertinged;
The armfuls are pack'd to the sagging mow.

I am there — I help — I came stretch'd
       atop of the load;
I felt its soft jolts — one leg reclined on the other;
I jump from the cross-beams, and seize
       the clover and timothy,
And roll head over heels, and tangle my hair
       full of wisps.

I am enamour'd of growing out-doors,
Of men that live among cattle,
    or taste of the ocean or woods,
Of the builders and steerers of ships,
    and the wielders of axes and mauls,
    and the drivers of horses;
I can eat and sleep with them
    week in and week out.

I am the poet of the woman
        the same as the man;
And I say it is as great to be
        a woman as to be a man;
And I say there is nothing
        greater than the mother
        of men.

I am he that walks with the
    tender and growing night;
I call to the earth and sea,
    half-held by the night.

Press close, bare-bosom'd night!
    Press close, magnetic,
    nourishing night!
Night of south winds! Night
    of the large few stars!
Still, nodding night!
    mad, naked, summer night.

Smile, O voluptuous, cool-breath'd earth!
Earth of the slumbering and liquid trees;
Earth of departed sunset! earth of the mountains,
            misty-topt!
Earth of the vitreous pour of the full moon, just
            tinged with blue!
Earth of shine and dark, mottling the tide of the river!
Earth of the limpid gray of clouds, brighter and clearer
            for my sake!
Far-swooping elbow'd earth! rich, apple-blossom'd earth!
Smile, for your lover comes!

You sea! I resign myself to you also — I guess
        what you mean;
I behold from the beach your crooked inviting fingers;
I believe you refuse to go back without feeling of me;
We must have a turn together — I undress — hurry
        me out of sight of the land;
Cushion me soft, rock me in billowy drowse;
Dash me with amorous wet — I can repay you.

Sea of stretch'd ground-swells!
Sea breathing broad and convulsive breaths!
Sea of the brine of life! sea of unshovell'd yet
        always-ready graves!
Howler and scooper of storms! capricious
        and dainty sea!
I am integral with you — I too am of one phase,
        and of all phases.

To behold the day-break!
The little light fades the immense and
       diaphanous shadows;
The air tastes good to my palate.
Hefts of the moving world, at innocent gambols, silently
       rising, freshly exuding,
Scooting obliquely high and low.
Something I cannot see puts upward libidinous prongs;
Seas of bright juice suffuse heaven.
The earth by the sky staid with — the daily close
       of their junction;
The heav'd challenge from the east that moment over
       my head;
The mocking taunt, See then whether you shall be
       master!

Dazzling and tremendous, how quick the sun-rise
       would kill me,
If I could not now and always send
       sun-rise out of me.

We also ascend, dazzling and tremendous
       as the sun;
We found our own, O my Soul, in the calm and cool
       of daybreak.

I think I will do nothing now but listen,
To accrue what I hear into myself — to let sounds
      contribute toward me.
I hear bravuras of birds, bustle of growing wheat,
      gossip of flames, clack of sticks
      cooking my meals;
I hear the sound I love, the sound of the human voice;
I hear all sounds running together, combined,
      fused or following;
Sounds of the city, and sounds out of the city —
      sounds of the day and night;
Talkative young ones to those that like them —

the loud laugh of work-people at
        their meals;
The angry base of disjointed friendship — the faint
        tones of the sick;
The judge with hands tight to the desk, his
        pallid lips pronouncing a
        death-sentence;
The heav'e'yo of stevedores unlading ships by
        the wharves —the refrain of the anchor-lifters;
The ring of alarm-bells — the cry of fire — the whirr
        of swift-streaking engines and hose-carts,
        with premonitory tinkles, and color'd lights;

The steam-whistle — the solid roll of the
       train of approaching cars;
The slow march play'd at the head of the
       association, marching two and two,
(They go to guard some corpse — the flag-tops
       are draped with black muslin.)
I hear the violoncello ('tis the young man's
       heart's complaint;)
I hear the key'd cornet — it glides quickly in
       through my ears;
It shakes mad-sweet pangs through
       my belly and breast.
I hear the chorus — it is a grand opera;
Ah, this indeed is music! This suits me.

A tenor large and fresh as the creation fills me;
The orbic flex of his mouth is pouring and filling me full.

I hear the train'd soprano — (what work, with hers, is this?)
The orchestra whirls me wider than Uranus flies;
It wrenches such ardors from me, I did not know I possess'd them;

It sails me — I dab with bare feet — they are lick'd by the
      indolent waves;
I am exposed, cut by bitter and angry hail — I lose my breath,
Steep'd amid honey'd morphine, my windpipe throttled in fakes of death;
At length let up again to feel the puzzle of puzzles,
And that we call BEING.

I think I could turn and live with animals, they
      are so placid and self-contain'd;
I stand and look at them long and long.

They do not sweat and whine about their condition;
They do not lie awake in the dark and weep for
       their sins;
They do not make me sick discussing their duty to God;
Not one is dissatisfied — not one is demented with
       the mania of owning things;
Not one kneels to another, nor to his kind that
       lived thousands of years ago;
Not one is respectable or industrious over the
       whole earth.
So they show their relations to me, and I accept them;
They bring me tokens of myself — they evince them plainly in their possession.

I wonder where they get those tokens:
Did I pass that way huge times ago, and negligently drop them?
Myself moving forward then and now and forever,

Gathering and showing more always and with velocity,
Infinite and omnigenous, and the like of these among them;
Not too exclusive toward the reachers of my remembrancers;
Picking out here one that I love, and now go with him on
        brotherly terms.

My ties and ballasts leave me — I travel — I sail — my elbows rest
      in the sea-gaps;
I skirt the sierras — my palms cover continents;
I am afoot with my vision.

By the city's quadrangular houses — in log huts — camping with lumbermen;
Along the ruts of the turnpike — along the dry gulch and rivulet bed;
Weeding my onion-patch, or hoeing rows of carrots and parsnips — crossing
      savannas — trailing in forests;
Prospecting — gold-digging — girdling the trees of a new purchase;
Scorch'd ankle-deep by the hot sand — hauling my boat down the
      shallow river;
Where the panther walks to and fro on a limb overhead — where the
      buck turns furiously at the hunter;
Where the rattlesnake suns his flabby length on a rock — where the otter
      is feeding on fish;
Where the alligator in his tough pimples sleeps by the bayou;
Where the black bear is searching for roots or honey — where the beaver
      pats the mud with his paddle-shaped tail;
Over the growing sugar — over the yellow-flower'd cotton plant — over
      the rice in its low moist field;
Over the sharp-peak'd farm house, with its scallop'd scum and slender
      shoots from the gutters;
Over the western persimmon — over the long-leav'd corn — over the
      delicate blue-flower flax;
Over the white and brown buckwheat, a hummer and buzzer there
      with the rest;
Over the dusky green of the rye as it ripples and shades in the breeze;
Scaling mountains, pulling myself cautiously up, holding on by low
      scragged limbs;
Walking the path worn in the grass, and beat through the leaves of
      the brush;
Where the quail is whistling betwixt the woods and the wheatlot;
Where the bat flies in the Seventh-month eve — where the great gold-bug
      drops through the dark;
Where flails keep time on the barn floor;
Where the brook puts out of the roots of the old tree and flows to the
      meadow;
Where cattle stand and shake away flies with the tremulous shuddering of
      their hides;
Where the cheese-cloth hangs in the kitchen — where andirons straddle the
      hearth-slab — where cobwebs fall in festoons from the rafters;
Where trip-hammers crash — where the press is whirling its cylinders;
Wherever the human heart beats with terrible throes under its ribs;

Where the pear-shaped balloon is floating aloft, (floating in it myself,
    and looking composedly down;)
Where the life-car is drawn on the slip-noose — where the heat hatches
    pale-green eggs in the dented sand;
Where the she-whale swims with her calf, and never forsakes it;
Where the steam-ship trails hind-ways its long pennant of smoke;
Where the fin of the shark cuts like a black chip out of the water;
Where the half-burn'd brig is riding on unknown currents,
Where shells grow to her slimy deck — where the dead are corrupting
    below;

Where the dense-starr'd flag is borne at the head of the regiments;
Approaching Manhattan, up by the long-stretching island;
Under Niagara, the cataract falling like a veil over my countenance;
Upon a door-step — upon the horse-block of hard wood outside;
Upon the race-course, or enjoying picnics or jigs, or a good game of
    base-ball;
At he-festivals, with blackguard jibes, ironical license, bull-dances, drinking,
    laughter;
At the cider-mill, tasting the sweets of the brown mash, sucking the
    juice through a straw;
At apple-peelings, wanting kisses for all the red fruit I find;
At musters, beach-parties, friendly bees, huskings, house-raisings:
Where the mocking-bird sounds his delicious gurgles, cackles, screams, weeps;
Where the hay-rick stands in the barn-yard — where the dry-stalks are
    scattered — where the brood-cow waits in the hovel;
Where the bull advances to do his masculine work — where the stud to
    the mare — where the cock is treading the hen;
Where the heifers browse — where geese nip their food with short jerks;
Where sun-down shadows lengthen over the limitless and lonesome prairie;
Where herds of buffalo make a crawling spread of the square miles far
    and near;
Where the humming-bird shimmers — where the neck of the long-lived
    swan is curving and winding;
Where the laughing-gull scoots by the shore, where she laughs her
    near-human laugh;
Where bee-hives range on a gray bench in the garden, half hid by the
    high weeds;
Where band-neck'd partridges roost in a ring on the ground with their
    heads out;
Where burial coaches enter the arch'd gates of a cemetery;
Where winter wolves bark amid wastes of snow and icicled trees;

Where the yellow-crown'd heron comes to the edge of the marsh at night
            and feeds upon small crabs;
Where the splash of swimmers and divers cools the warm noon;
Where the katy-did works her chromatic reed on the walnut-tree over
        the well;
Through patches of citrons and cucumbers with silver-wired leaves;
Through the salt-lick or orange glade, or under conical firs;
Through the gymnasium — through the curtain'd saloon — through the
            office or public hall;
Pleas'd with the native, and pleas'd with the foreign — pleas'd with
            the new and old;
Pleas'd with women, the homely as well as the handsome;
Pleas'd with the quakeress as she puts off her bonnet and talks melodiously;
Pleas'd with the tune of the choir of the white-wash'd church;
Pleas'd with the earnest words of the sweating Methodist preacher, or any
            preacher — impress'd seriously at the camp-meeting:
Looking in at the shop-windows of Broadway the whole forenoon — flatting
            the flesh of my nose on the thick plate-glass;
Wandering the same afternoon with my face turn'd up to the clouds,
My right and left arms round the sides of two friends, and I in the
            middle:
Coming home with the silent and dark-cheek'd bush-boy — (behind me
            he rides at the drape of the day;)
Far from the settlements, studying the print of animals' feet, or the
            moccasin print;
By the cot in the hospital, reaching lemonade to a feverish patient;
Nigh the coffin'd corpse when all is still, examining with a candle:
Voyaging to every port, to dicker and adventure;
Hurrying with the modern crowd, as eager and fickle as any;
Hot toward one I hate, ready in my madness to knife him;
Solitary at midnight in my back yard, my thoughts gone from me a
            long while;
Walking the old hills of Judea, with the beautiful gentle God by my side;
Speeding through space — speeding through heaven and the stars;

Speeding amid the seven satellites, and the broad ring, and the diameter
            of eighty thousand miles;
Speeding with tail'd meteors — throwing fire-balls like the rest;
Carrying the crescent child that carries its own full mother in its belly;
Storming, enjoying, planning, loving, cautioning,
Backing and filling, appearing and disappearing;
I tread day and night such roads.

I visit the orchards of spheres, and look at
      the product:
And look at quintillions ripen'd, and look
      at quintillions green.

I fly the flight of the fluid and swallowing soul;
My course runs below the soundings of plummets.

I help myself to material and immaterial;
No guard can shut me off, nor law prevent me.

I anchor my ship for a little while only;

My messengers continually cruise away, or bring their returns to me.

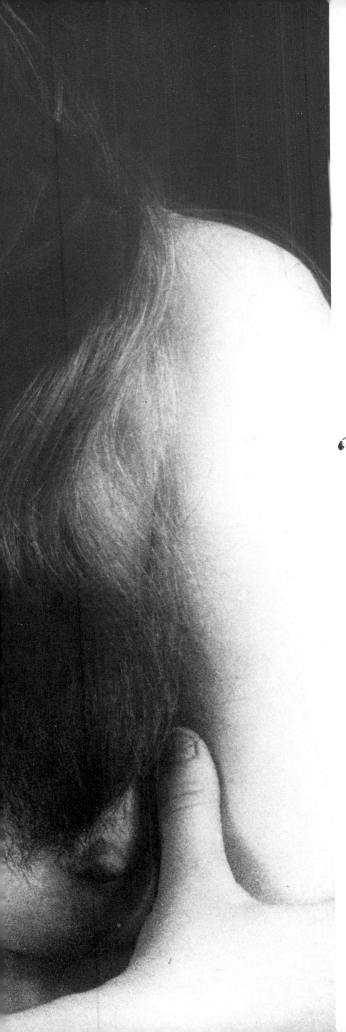

Excerpts from "I Sing the Body Electric"

I sing the Body electric;
The armies of those I love engirth me,
      and I engirth them;
They will not let me off till I go with them,
      respond to them,
And discorrupt them, and charge them full
      with the charge of the Soul.

Was it doubted that those who corrupt
      their own bodies conceal themselves?
And if those who defile the living
      are as bad as they who defile the dead?
And if the body does not do as much
      as the Soul?
And if the body were not the Soul,
      what is the Soul?

The love of the Body of man or woman
      balks account — the body itself balks account;
That of the male is perfect, and that
      of the female is perfect.

The expression of the face balks account;
But the expression of a well-made man appears not only in his face;
It is in his limbs and joints also, it is curiously in the joints
      of his hips and wrists;
It is in his walk, the carriage of his neck, the flex of his waist and knees —
      dress does not hide him;
The strong, sweet, supple quality he has, strikes through the cotton
      and flannel;
To see him pass conveys as much as the best poem, perhaps more;
You linger to see his back, and the back of his neck and shoulder-side.

The sprawl and fulness of babes, the bosoms and heads of women,
      the folds of their dress, their style as we pass in the street,
      the contour of their shape downwards,
The swimmer naked in the swimming-bath, seen as he swims through the
      transparent green-shine, or lies with his face up, and rolls
      silently to and fro in the heave of the water,

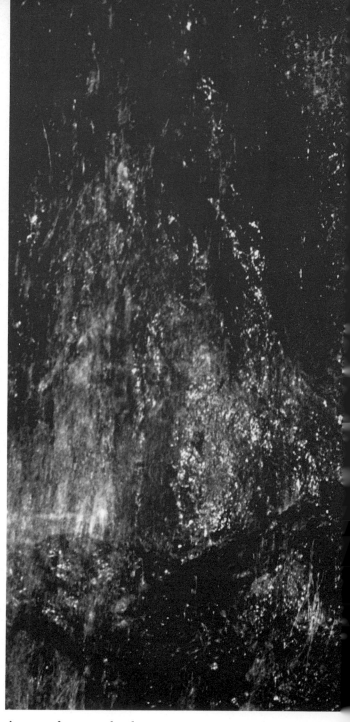

The bending forward and backward of rowers in row-boats, the horseman
        in his saddle,
Girls, mothers, housekeepers, in all their performances,
The group of laborers seated at noon-time with their open dinner-kettles,
        and their wives waiting,
The female soothing a child — the farmer's daughter in the garden
        or cow-yard,
The young fellow hoeing corn — the sleigh-driver guiding his six horses
        through the crowd,

The wrestle of wrestlers, two apprentice-boys, quite grown, lusty,
      good-natured, native-born, out on the vacant lot
      at sundown, after work,
The coats and caps thrown down, the embrace of love and resistance,
The upper-hold and the under-hold, the hair rumpled over and blinding the eyes;
The march of firemen in their own costumes, the play of masculine muscle
      through clean-setting trowsers and waiststraps,
The slow return from the fire, the pause when the bell strikes suddenly
      again, and the listening on the alert,

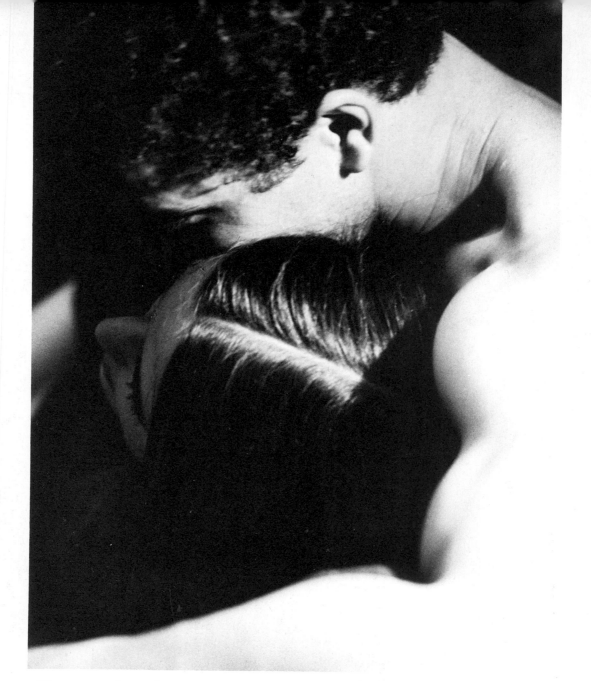

The natural, perfect, varied attitudes — the bent head, the curv'd neck,
     and the counting;
Such-like I love — I loosen myself, pass freely, am at the mother's breast
     with the little child,
Swim with the swimmers, wrestle with the wrestlers, march in line with
     the firemen, and pause, listen, and count.

"To Old Age"

I see in you the estuary that
enlarges and spreads itself grandly
as it pours in the great Sea.

Excerpts from "Song of the Broad-Axe"

The shapes arise!
Shapes of factories, arsenals, foundries, markets;
Shapes of the two-threaded tracks of railroads;
Shapes of the sleepers of bridges, vast frameworks,
      girders, arches;
Shapes of the fleets of barges, towns, lake and canal
      craft, river craft.

The shapes arise!
Ship-yards and dry-docks along the Eastern
     and Western Seas, and
     in many a bay and by-place,
The live-oak kelsons, the pine planks, the spars,
     the hackmatack-roots for knees,
The ships themselves on their ways, the tiers of
     scaffolds, the workmen busy outside and inside,
The tools lying around, the great augur and the little
     augur, the adze, bolt, line, square,
     gouge, and bead-plane.

The shapes arise!
The shape measur'd, saw'd, jack'd, join'd, stain'd,
The coffin-shape for the dead to lie within his shroud;
The shape got out in posts, in the bedstead posts,
      in the posts of the bride's bed;
The shape of the little trough, the shape
     of the rockers beneath,
      the shape of the babe's cradle;
The shape of the floor-planks, the floor-planks
     for dancers' feet;
The shape of the planks of the family home, the home
     of the friendly parents and children,
The shape of the roof of the home of the happy young man
     and woman — the roof over the
      well-married young man and woman,
The roof over the supper joyously cook'd by the chaste
     wife, and joyously eaten by the chaste
      husband, content after his day's work.

The main shapes arise!
Shapes of Democracy, total — result of centuries;
Shapes, ever projecting other shapes;
Shapes of turbulent manly cities;
Shapes of the friends and home-givers of the whole earth,
Shapes bracing the earth, and braced with the whole earth.

"Song of the Open Road"

1

Afoot and light-hearted, I take to the open road,
Healthy, free, the world before me,
The long brown path before me, leading wherever I choose.

Henceforth I whimper no more, postpone no more, need nothing
Henceforth I ask not good-fortune — I myself am good-fortune;
Strong and content, I travel the open road.

The earth — that is sufficient;
I do not want the constellations any nearer;
I know they are very well where they are;
I know they suffice for those who belong to them.

(Still here I carry my old delicious burdens;
I carry them, men and women — I carry them with me wherever I go;
I swear it is impossible for me to get rid of them;
I am fill'd with them, and I will fill them in return.)

2

You road I enter upon and look around I believe you are not all that is here;
I believe that much unseen is also here.

Here the profound lesson of reception, neither preference or denial;
The black with his woolly head, the felon, the diseas'd, the illiterate
      person, are not denied;
The birth, the hasting after the physician, the beggar's tramp, the
      drunkard's stagger, the laughing party of mechanics,
The escaped youth, the rich person's carriage, the fop, the eloping couple,
The early market man, the hearse, the moving of furniture into the town,
      the return back from the town.
They pass — I also pass — anything passes — none can be interdicted;
None but are accepted — none but are dear to me.

3

You air that serves me with breath to speak!
You objects that call from diffusion my meanings, and give them shape!
You light that wraps me and all things in delicate equable showers!
You paths worn in the irregular hollows by the roadsides!
I think you are latent with unseen existences — you are so dear to me.

You flagg'd walks of the cities! you strong curbs at the edges!
You ferries! you planks and posts of wharves! you timber-lined sides!
       you distant ships!
You rows of houses! you window-pierc'd facades! you roofs!
You porches and entrances! you copings and iron guards!
You windows whose transparent shells might expose so much!
You doors and ascending steps! you arches!
You gray stones of interminable pavements! you trodden crossings!
From all that has been near you, I believe you have imparted to yourselves,
       and now would impart the same secretly to me;
From the living and the dead I think you have peopled your impassive surfaces,
       and the spirits thereof would be evident and amicable with me.

4

The earth expanding right hand and left hand,
The picture alive, every part in its best light,
The music falling in where it is wanted, and stopping where it is not wanted,
The cheerful voice of the public road — the gay fresh sentiment of the road.
O highway I travel! O public road! do you say to me, *Do not leave me?*
Do you say, *Venture not? If you leave me, you are lost?*
Do you say, *I am already prepared — I am well-beaten and undenied — adhere to me?*

O public road! I say back, I am not afraid to leave you — yet I love you;
You express me better than I can express myself;
You shall be more to me than my poem.
I think heroic deeds were all conceiv'd in the open air, and all great poems also;
I think I could stop here myself, and do miracles;
(My judgments, thoughts, I henceforth try by the open air, the road;)
I think whatever I shall meet on the road I shall like, and whoever beholds me
       shall like me;
I think whoever I see must be happy.

From this hour, freedom!
From this hour I ordain myself loos'd of limits and imaginary lines,
Going where I list, my own master, total and absolute,

Listening to others, and considering well what they say,
Pausing, searching, receiving, contemplating,
Gently, but with undeniable will, divesting myself of the holds that would hold me.

I inhale great draughts of space;
The east and the west are mine, and the north and the south are mine.

I am larger, better than I thought;
I did not know I held so much goodness
All seems beautiful to me;
I can repeat over to men and women, You have done such good to me, I would
        do the same to you.

I will recruit for myself and you as I go;
I will scatter myself among men and women as I go;
I will toss the new gladness and roughness among them;
Whoever denies me, it shall not trouble me;
Whoever accepts me, he or she shall be blessed, and shall bless me.

5

Now if a thousand perfect men were to appear, it would not amaze me;
Now if a thousand beautiful forms of women appear'd, it would not astonish me.

Now I see the secret of the making of the best persons,
It is to grow in the open air, and to eat and sleep with the earth.

Here a great personal deed has room;
A great deed seizes upon the hearts of the whole race of men,
Its effusion of strength and will overwhelms law, and mocks all authority
        and all argument against it.

Here is the test of wisdom;
Wisdom is not finally tested in schools;
Wisdom cannot be pass'd from one having it, to another not having it;
Wisdom is of the Soul, is not susceptible of proof, is its own proof,
Applies to all stages and objects and qualities, and is content,
Is the certainty of the reality and immortality of things, and the
        excellence of things;
Something there is in the float of the sight of things that provokes it out
        of the Soul.
Now I reëxamine philosophies and religions,
They may prove well in lecture-rooms, yet not prove at all under the spacious
        clouds, and along the landscape and flowing currents.

Here is realization;

Here is a man tallied — he realizes here what he has in him;
The past, the future, majesty, love — if they are vacant of you, you are
vacant of them.

Only the kernel of every object nourishes;
Where is he who tears off the husks for you and me?
Where is he that undoes stratagems and envelopes for you and me?

Here is adhesiveness — it is not previously fashion'd — it is apropos;
Do you know what it is, as you pass, to be loved by strangers?
Do you know the talk of those turning eye-balls?

7

Here is the efflux of the Soul;
The efflux of the Soul comes from within, through embower'd gates, ever
provoking questions:
These yearnings, why are they? These thoughts in the darkness, why are they?
Why are there men and women that while they are nigh me, the sun-light
expands my blood?
Why, when they leave me, do my pennants of joy sink flat and lank?
Why are there trees I never walk under, but large and melodious thoughts
descend upon me?
(I think they hang there winter and summer on those trees, and always
drop fruit as I pass;)
What is it I interchange so suddenly with strangers?
What with some driver, as I ride on the seat by his side?
What with some fisherman, drawing his seine by the shore, as I walk by,
and pause?
What gives me to be free to a woman's or man's good-will?
What gives them to be free to mine?

8

The efflux of the Soul is happiness — here is happiness;
I think it pervades the open air, waiting at all times;
Now it flows unto us — we are rightly charged.

Here rises the fluid and attaching character;
The fluid and attaching character is the freshness and sweetness of
man and woman;
(The herbs of the morning sprout no fresher and sweeter every day out of the
roots of themselves, than it sprouts fresh and sweet
continually out of itself.)

Toward the fluid and attaching character exudes the sweat of the love of
young and old;
From it falls distill'd the charm that mocks beauty and attainments;
Toward it heaves the shuddering longing ache of contact.

9

Allons! whoever you are, come travel with me!
Traveling with me, you find what never tires.

The earth never tires;
The earth is rude, silent, incomprehensible at first — Nature is rude and
      incomprehensible at first;
Be not discouraged — keep on — there are divine things, well envelop'd;
I swear to you there are divine things more beautiful than words can tell.

Allons! we must not stop here!
However sweet these laid-up stores — however convenient this dwelling, we
      cannot remain here;
However shelter'd this port, and however calm these waters, we must not
      anchor here;
However welcome the hospitality that surrounds us, we are permitted to
      receive it but a little while.

10

Allons! the inducements shall be greater;
We will sail pathless and wild seas;
We will go where winds blow, waves dash, and the Yankee clipper speeds by
      under full sail.

Allons! with power, liberty, the earth, the elements!
Health, defiance, gayety, self-esteem, curiosity;
Allons! from all formules!
From your formules, O bat-eyed and materialistic priests!

The stale cadaver blocks up the passage— the burial waits no longer.

Allons! yet take warning!
He traveling with me needs the best blood, thews, endurance;
None may come to the trial, till he or she bring courage and health.

Come not here if you have already spent the best of yourself;
Only those may come, who come in sweet and determin'd bodies;
No diseas'd person — no rum-drinker or venereal taint is permitted here,

I and mine do not convince by arguments, similes, rhymes;
We convince by our presence.

11

Listen! I will be honest with you;
I do not offer the old smooth prizes, but offer rough new prizes;
These are the days that must happen to you:

You shall not heap up what is call'd riches,
You shall scatter with lavish hand all that you earn or achieve,
You but arrive at the city to which you were destin'd — you hardly settle

yourself to satisfaction, before you are called by an
      irresistible call to depart,
You shall be treated to the ironical smiles and mockings of those
      who remain behind you;
What beckonings of love you receive, you shall only answer with
      passionate kisses of parting,
You shall not allow the hold of those who spread their reach'd
      hands toward you.

12

Allons! after the GREAT COMPANIONS! and to belong to them!
They too are on the road! they are the swift majestic men!
      they are greatest women.

Over that which hinder'd them — over that which retarded —
      passing impediments large or small,
Committers of crimes, committers of many beautiful virtues,
Enjoyers of calms of seas, and storms of seas,
Sailors of many a ship, walkers of many a mile of land,
Habitués of many distant countries, habitués of far-distant
      dwellings,
Trusters of men and women, observers of cities, solitary toilers,
Pausers and contemplators of tufts, blossoms, shells of the shore,
Dancers at wedding dances, kissers of brides, tender helpers of
      children, bearers of children,
Soldiers of revolts, standers by gaping graves, lowerers down of coffins,
Journeyers over consecutive seasons, over the years — the curious
      years, each emerging from that which preceded it,
Journeyers as with companions, namely, their own diverse phases,
Forth-steppers from the latent unrealized baby-days,
Journeyers gayly with their own youth — Journeyers with their
      bearded and well-grain'd manhood,
Journeyers with their womanhood, ample, unsurpass'd, content,
Journeyers with their own sublime old age of manhood or womanhood,
Old age, calm, expanded, broad with the haughty breadth of
      the universe,
Old age, flowing free with the delicious near-by freedom of death.

13

Allons! to that which is endless, as it was beginningless,
To undergo much, tramps of days, rests of nights,
To merge all in the travel they tend to, and the days and nights
      they tend to,
Again to merge them in the start of superior journeys;

To see nothing anywhere but what you may reach it and pass it,
To conceive no time, however distant, but what you may reach it
and pass it,
To look up or down no road but it stretches and waits for you —
however long, but it stretches and waits for you;
To see no being, not God's or any. but you also go thither,
To see no possession but you may possess it — enjoying all without labor or
purchase — abstracting the feast, yet not abstracting
one particle of it;
To take the best of the farmer's farm and the rich man's elegant villa,
and the chaste blessings of the well-married couple, and the fruits
of orchards and flowers of gardens,
To take to your use out of the compact cities as you pass through,
To carry buildings and streets with you afterward wherever you go,
To gather the minds of men out of their brains as you encounter them — to
gather the love out of their hearts,
To take your lovers on the road with you, for all that you leave them
behind you,
To know the universe itself as a road — as many roads — as roads for
traveling souls.

14

The Soul travels;
The body does not travel as much as the soul;
The body has just as great a work as the soul, and parts away at last for
the journeys of the soul.

All parts away for the progress of souls;
All religion, all solid things, arts, governments, — all that was or is
apparent upon this globe or any globe, falls into niches and corners
before the procession of Souls along the grand roads of the universe.

Of the progress of the souls of men and women along the grand roads of the
universe, all other progress is the needed emblem and sustenance.

Forever alive, forever forward,
Stately, solemn, sad, withdrawn, baffled, mad, turbulent, feeble, dissatisfied,
Desperate, proud, fond, sick, accepted by men, rejected by men,
They go! they go! I know that they go, but I know not where they go;
But I know that they go toward the best — toward something great.

15

Allons! whoever you are! come forth!
You must not stay sleeping and dallying there in the house,
though you built it, or though it has been built for you.

Allons! out of the dark confinement!
It is useless to protest — I know all, and expose it.

Behold, through you as bad as the rest,
Through the laughter, dancing, dining, supping, of people,
Inside of dresses and ornaments, inside of those wash'd and trimm'd faces,
Behold a secret silent loathing and despair.

No husband, no wife, no friend, trusted to hear the confession;
Another self, a duplicate of everyone, skulking and hiding it goes,
Formless and wordless through the streets of the cities, polite and bland
   in the parlors,
In the cars of railroads, in steamboats, in the public assembly,
Home to the houses of men and women, at the table, in the bed-room, everywhere,
Smartly attired, countenance smiling, form upright, death under the breastbones,
   hell under the skull-bones,
Under the broadcloth and gloves, under the ribbons and artificial flowers,
Keeping fair with the customs, speaking not a syllable of itself,
Speaking of anything else, but never of itself.

16

Allons! through struggles and wars!
The goal that was named cannot be countermanded.

Have the past struggles succeeded?
What has succeeded? yourself? your nation? nature?
Now understand me well — It is provided in the essence of things, that from
   any fruition of success, no matter what, shall come forth something
   to make a greater struggle necessary.

My call is the call of battle — I nourish active rebellion;
He going with me must go well arm'd;
He going with me goes often with spare diet, poverty, angry enemies, desertions.

17

Allons! the road is before us!
It is safe — I have tried it — my own feet have tried it well.

Allons! be not detain'd!
Let the paper remain on the desk unwritten, and the book on the shelf unopen'd!
Let the tools remain in the workshop! let the money remain unearn'd!
Let the school stand! mind not the cry of the teacher!
Let the preacher preach in his pulpit! let the lawyer plead in the court,
   and the judge expound the law.

Mon enfant! I give you my hand!
I give you my love, more precious than money,
I give you myself, before preaching or law;
Will you give me yourself? will you come travel with me?
Shall we stick by each other as long as we live?

Excerpts from "Faces"

Sauntering the pavement, or riding the country by-road — lo!
        such faces!
Faces of friendship, precision, caution, suavity, ideality;
The spiritual, prescient face — the always welcome,
        common, benevolent face,
The face of the singing of music — the grand faces of natural
        lawyers and judges, broad at the back-top;
The faces of hunters and fishers, bulged at the brows — the
        shaved blanch'd faces of orthodox citizens;
The pure, extravagant, yearning, questioning artist's face;
The ugly face of some beautiful Soul, the handsome detested
        or despised face;
The sacred faces of infants, the illuminated face of the mother
        of many children;
The face of an amour, the face of veneration;
The face as of a dream, the face of an immobile rock;
The face withdrawn of its good and bad, a castrated face;
A wild hawk, his wings clipped by the clipper;
A stallion that yielded at last to the thongs and knife of the gelder.

Sauntering the pavement, thus, or crossing the ceaseless ferry,
        faces, and faces, and faces:
I see them, and complain not, and am content with all. . . .

The Lord advances, and yet advances;
Always the shadow in front — always the reach'd hand
    bringing up the laggards.

Out of this face emerge banners and horses —O superb! I see
    what is coming;
I see the high pioneer-caps — I see the staves of runners
    clearing the way,
I hear victorious drums.

This face is a life-boat;
This is the face commanding and bearded, it asks no odds
       for the rest;
This face is flavor'd fruit, ready for eating;
This face of a healthy honest boy is the programme
       of all good.
These faces bear testimony, slumbering or awake;
They show their descent from the Master himself.

Off the word I have spoken, I except not one — red,
       white, black, are all deific;
In each house is the ovum — it comes forth after a
       thousand years.
Spots or cracks at the window do not disturb me;
Tall and sufficient stand behind, and make signs to me;
I read the promise, and patiently wait.

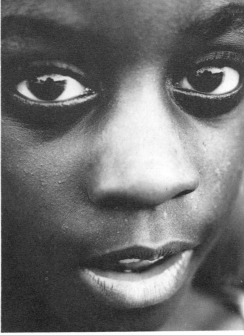

"Pioneers! O Pioneers!"

Come, my tan-faced children,
Follow well in order, get your weapons ready;
Have you your pistols? have you your sharp edged axes?
      Pioneers! O pioneers!

For we cannot tarry here,
We must march my darlings, we must bear the brunt of danger,
We, the youthful sinewy races, all the rest on us depend,
      Pioneers! O pioneers!

O you youths, western youths,
So impatient, full of action, full of manly pride and friendship,
Plain I see you, western youths, see you tramping with the foremost,
      Pioneers! O pioneers!

Have the elder races halted?
Do they droop and end their lesson, wearied, over there beyond the seas?
We take up the task eternal, and the burden, and the lesson,
      Pioneers! O pioneers!

All the past we leave behind;
We debouch upon a newer, mightier world, varied world;
Fresh and strong the world we seize, world of labor and the march,
      Pioneers! O pioneers!

We detachments steady throwing,
Down the edges, through the passes, up the mountains steep,
Conquering, holding, daring, venturing, as we go, the unknown ways,
      Pioneers! O pioneers!

We primeval forests felling,
We the rivers stemming, vexing we, and piercing deep the mines within;
We the surface broad surveying, we the virgin soil upheaving,
      Pioneers! O pioneers!

Colorado men are we,
From the peaks gigantic, from the great sierras and the high plateaus,
From the mine and from the gully, from the hunting trail we come,
      Pioneers! O pioneers!

From Nebraska, from Arkansas,
Central inland race are we, from Missouri, with the continental blood intervein'd;
All the hands of comrades clasping, all the Southern, all the Northern,
      Pioneers! O pioneers!

O resistless, restless race!
O beloved race in all! O my breast aches with tender love for all!
O I mourn and yet exult — I am rapt with love for all,
      Pioneers! O pioneers!

Raise the mighty mother mistress,
Waving high the delicate mistress, over all the starry mistress,
      (bend your heads all,)
Raise the fang'd and warlike mistress, stern, impassive, weapon'd mistress,
      Pioneers! O pioneers!

See my children, resolute children,
By those swarms upon our rear, we must never yield or falter,
Ages back in ghostly millions, frowning there behind us urging,
      Pioneers! O pioneers!

On and on, the compact ranks,
With accessions ever waiting, with the places of the dead quickly fill'd,
Through the battle, through defeat, moving yet and never stopping,
      Pioneers! O pioneers!

O to die advancing on!
Are there some of us to droop and die? has the hour come?
Then upon the march we fittest die, soon and sure the gap is fill'd,
      Pioneers! O pioneers!

All the pulses of the world,
Falling in, they beat for us, with the western movement beat;
Holding single or together, steady moving, to the front, all for us,
      Pioneers! O pioneers!

Life's involv'd and varied pageants,
All the forms and shows, all the workmen at their work,
All the seamen and the landsmen, all the masters with their slaves,
      Pioneers! O pioneers!

All the hapless silent lovers,
All the prisoners in the prisons, all the righteous and the wicked,
All the joyous, all the sorrowing, all the living, all the dying,
      Pioneers! O pioneers!

I too with my soul and body,
We, a curious trio, picking, wandering on our way,
Through these shores, amid the shadows, with the apparitions pressing,
  Pioneers! O pioneers!

Lo! the darting bowling orb!
Lo! the brother orbs around! all the clustering suns and planets;
All the dazzling days, all the mystic nights with dreams,
  Pioneers! O pioneers!

These are of us, they are with us,
All for primal needed work, while the followers there in embryo wait behind,
We to-day's procession heading, we the route for travel clearing,
  Pioneers! O pioneers!

O you daughters of the west!
O you young and elder daughters! O you mothers and you wives!
Never must you be divided, in our ranks you move united,
  Pioneers! O pioneers!

Minstrels latent on the prairies!
(Shrouded bards of other lands! you may sleep — you have done your work;)
Soon I hear you coming warbling, soon you rise and tramp amid us,
  Pioneers! O pioneers!

Not for delectations sweet;
Not the cushion and the slipper, not the peaceful and the studious;
Not the riches safe and palling, not for us the tame enjoyment,
  Pioneers! O pioneers!

Do the feasters gluttonous feast?
Do the corpulent sleepers sleep? have they lock'd and bolted doors?
Still be ours the diet hard, and the blanket on the ground,
  Pioneers! O pioneers!

Has the night descended?
Was the road of late so toilsome? did we stop discouraged, nodding on our way?
Yet a passing hour I yield you, in your tracks to pause oblivious,
  Pioneers! O pioneers!

Till with sound of trumpet,
Far, far off the day-break call — hark! how loud and clear I hear it wind;
Swift! to the head of the army! – swift! spring to your places,
  Pioneers! O pioneers!

"Song at Sunset"

Splendor of ended day, floating and filling me!
Hour prophetic — hour resuming the past!
Inflating my throat — you, divine average!
You, Earth and Life, till the last ray gleams, I sing.

Open mouth of my Soul, uttering gladness,
Eyes of my Soul, seeing perfection,
Natural life of me, faithfully praising things;
Corroborating forever the triumph of things.

Illustrious every one!
Illustrious what we name space — sphere of unnumber'd spirits;
Illustrious the mystery of motion, in all beings, even the tiniest insect;
Illustrious the attribute of speech — the senses — the body;
Illustrious the passing light! Illustrious the pale reflection
    on the new moon in the western sky!
Illustrious whatever I see, or hear, or touch, to the last.

Good in all,
In the satisfaction and aplomb of animals,
In the annual return of the seasons,
In the hilarity of youth,
In the strength and flush of manhood,
In the grandeur and exquisiteness of old age,
In the superb vistas of Death.

Wonderful to depart;
Wonderful to be here!
The heart, to jet the all-alike and innocent blood!
To breathe the air, how delicious!
To speak! to walk! to seize something by the hand!
To prepare for sleep, for bed — to look on my rose-color'd flesh;
To be conscious of my body, so satisfied, so large;
To be this incredible God I am;
To have gone forth among other Gods — these men and women I love.

Wonderful how I celebrate you and myself!
How my thoughts play subtly at the spectacles around!
How the clouds pass silently overhead!
How the earth darts on and on! and how the sun, moon, stars, dart on and on!
How the water sports and sings! (Surely it is alive!)
How the trees rise and stand up — with strong trunks — with branches and leaves!
(Surely there is something more in each of the trees — some living Soul.)

O amazement of things! even the least particle!
O·spirituality of things!
O strain musical, flowing through ages and continents — now reaching me and America!
I take your strong chords — I intersperse them, and cheerfully pass them forward.

I too carol the sun, usher'd, or at noon, or, as now, setting,
I too throb to the brain and beauty of the earth, and of all the growths of the earth,
I too have felt the resistless call of myself.

As I sail'd down the Mississippi,
As I wander'd over the prairies,
As I have lived — As I have look'd through my windows, my eyes,
As I went forth in the morning — As I beheld the light breaking in the east;
As I bathed on the beach of the Eastern Sea, and again on the beach of the Western Sea;
As I roam'd the streets of inland Chicago — whatever streets I have roam'd;
Or cities, or silent woods, or peace, or even amid the sights of war;
Wherever I have been, I have charged myself with contentment and triumph.

I sing the Equalities, modern or old,
I sing the endless finales of things;
I say Nature continues — Glory continues;
I praise with electric voice;
For I do not see one imperfection in the universe;
And I do not see one cause or result lamentable at last in the universe.

O setting sun! though the time has come,
I still warble under you, if none else does, unmitigated adoration.

Excerpts from "When Lilacs Last in the Door-yard Bloom'd"

When lilacs last in the door-yard bloom'd,
And the great star early droop'd in the western sky in the night,
I mourn'd — and yet shall mourn with ever-returning spring.

O ever-returning spring! trinity sure to me you bring;
Lilac blooming perennial, and drooping star in the west,
And thought of him I love.

O powerful, western, fallen star!
O shades of night! O moody, tearful night!
O great star disappear'd! O the black murk that hides the star!
O cruel hands that hold me powerless! O helpless soul of me!
O harsh surrounding cloud, that will not free my soul!

In the door-yard fronting an old farm-house, near the white-
      wash'd palings,
Stands the lilac bush, tall-growing, with heart-shaped leaves of
      rich green,
With many a pointed blossom, rising, delicate, with the perfume
      strong I love,
With every leaf a miracle . . . . . and from this bush in the door-yard
With delicate-color'd blossoms, and heart-shaped leaves of rich green,
A sprig, with its flower, I break.

In the swamp, in secluded recesses,
A shy and hidden bird is warbling a song.

Solitary, the thrush,
The hermit, withdrawn to himself, avoiding the settlements,
Sings by himself a song.

Song of the bleeding throat!
Death's outlet song of life — (for well, dear brother, I know,
If thou wast not gifted to sing, thou would'st surely die.)

Over the breast of the spring, the land, amid cities,
Amid lanes, and through old woods, (where lately the violets
          peep'd from the ground, spotting the gray debris;)
Amid the grass in the fields each side of the lanes — passing the
          endless grass;
Passing the yellow-spear'd wheat, every grain from its shroud in
          the dark-brown fields uprising;
Passing the apple-tree blows of white and pink in the orchards;
Carrying a corpse to where it shall rest in the grave,
Night and day journeys a coffin.

Coffin that passes through lanes and streets,
Through day and night, with the great cloud darkening the land,
With the pomp of the inloop'd flags, with the cities draped in black,
With the show of the States themselves, as of crape-veil'd women, standing,
With processions long and winding, and the flambeaus of the night,
With the countless torches lit — with the silent sea of faces,
          and the unbared heads,
With the waiting depot, the arriving coffin, and the sombre faces,
With dirges through the night, with the thousand voices rising
          strong and solemn;
With all the mournful voices of the dirges, pour'd around the coffin,
The dim-lit churches and the shuddering organs — Where amid
          these you journey,
With the tolling, tolling bells' perpetual clang;
Here! coffin that slowly passes,
I give you my sprig of lilac.

(Nor for you, for one, alone;
Blossoms and branches green to coffins all I bring:
For fresh as the morning — thus would I carol a song for you, O
          sane and sacred death.

All over bouquets of roses,
O death! I cover you over with roses and early lilies;
But mostly and now the lilac that blooms the first,
Copious, I break, I break the sprigs from the bushes;
With loaded arms I come, pouring for you,
For you, and the coffins all of you, O death.)

O western orb, sailing the heaven!
Now I know what you must have meant, as a month since we walk'd,
As we walk'd up and down in the dark blue so mystic,
As we walk'd in silence the transparent shadowy night,
As I saw you had something to tell, as you bent to me night
        after night,
As you droop'd from the sky low down, as if to my side,
        (while the other stars all look'd on;)
As we wander'd together the solemn night, (for something, I
        know not what, kept me from sleep;)
As the night advanced, and I saw on the rim of the west, ere you
        went, how full you were of woe;
As I stood on the rising ground in the breeze, in the cold
        transparent night,
As I watch'd where you pass'd and was lost in the netherward
        black of the night,
As my soul, in its trouble, dissatisfied, sank, as where you,
        sad orb,
Concluded, dropt in the night, and was gone.

Sing on, there in the swamp!
O singer bashful and tender! I hear your notes — I hear your call;
I hear — I come presently — I understand you;
But a moment I linger — for the lustrous star has detain'd me;
The star, my departing comrade, holds and detains me.

O how shall I warble myself for the dead one there I loved?
And how shall I deck my song for the large sweet soul that has gone?
And what shall my perfume be, for the grave of him I love?

Sea-winds, blown from east and west,
Blown from the eastern sea, and blown from the western sea,
        till there on the prairies meeting:
These, and with these, and the breath of my chant,
I perfume the grave of him I love.

O what shall I hang on the chamber walls?
And what shall the pictures be that I hang on the walls,
To adorn the burial-house of him I love?

Pictures of growing spring, and farms, and homes,
With the Fourth-month eve at sundown, and the gray smoke
        lucid and bright,
With floods of the yellow gold of the gorgeous, indolent,
        sinking sun, burning, expanding the air;
With the fresh sweet herbage under foot, and the pale green
        leaves of the trees prolific;
In the distance the flowing glaze, the breast of the river,
        with a wind-dapple here and there;
With ranging hills on the banks, with many a line against the
        sky, and shadow;
And the city at hand, with dwellings so dense, and stacks of
        chimneys,
And all the scenes of life, and the workshops, and the workmen
        homeward returning.

Lo! body and soul! this land!
Mighty Manhattan, with spires, and the sparkling and hurrying
        tides, and the ships;
The varied and ample land — the South and the North in the
        light-Ohio's shores, and flashing Missouri,
And ever the far-spreading prairies, cover'd with grass and corn.

Lo! the most excellent sun, so calm and haughty;
The violet and purple morn, with just-felt breezes;
The gentle, soft-born, measureless light;
The miracle, spreading, bathing all — the fulfill'd noon;
The coming eve, delicious — the welcome night, and the stars,
Over my cities shining all, enveloping man and land.

Sing on! sing on, you gray-brown bird!
Sing from the swamps, the recesses — pour your chant from the bushes;
Limitless out of the dusk, out of the cedars and pines.

Sing on, dearest brother — warble your reedy song;
Loud human song, with voice of uttermost woe.

O liquid, and free, and tender!
O wild and loose to my soul! O wondrous singer!
You only I hear . . . . . . yet the star holds me, (but will soon depart;)
Yet the lilac, with mastering odor, holds me.

"O Captain! My Captain!"

O Captain! my Captain! our fearful trip is done;
The ship has weather'd every rack, the prize we sought is won;
The port is near, the bells I hear, the people all exulting,
While follow eyes the steady keel, the vessel grim and daring:
      But O heart! heart! heart!
        O the bleeding drops of red,
          Where on the deck my Captain lies,
           Fallen cold and dead.

2

O Captain! my Captain! rise up and hear the bells;
Rise up — for you the flag is flung — for you the bugle trills;
For you bouquets and ribbon'd wreaths — for you the shores a-crowding;
For you they call, the swaying mass, their eager faces turning;
      Here Captain! dear father!
        This arm beneath your head;
          It is some dream that on the deck,
           You've fallen cold and dead.

3

My Captain does not answer, his lips are pale and still;
My father does not feel my arm, he has no pulse nor will;
The ship is anchor'd safe and sound, its voyage closed and done;
From fearful trip, the victor ship, comes in with object won:
      Exult, O shores, and ring, O bells!
        But I, with mournful tread,
          Walk the deck my Captain lies,
           Fallen cold and dead.

"A Carol of Harvest"

1

A song of the good green grass!
A song no more of the city streets;
A song of farms — a song of the soil of fields.

A song with the smell of sun-dried hay, where the
        nimble pitchers handle the pitch-fork;
A song tasting of new wheat, and of fresh-husk'd maize.

2

For the lands, for these passionate days, for myself,
Now I awhile return to thee, O soil of Autumn fields,
Reclining on thy breast, giving myself to thee,
Answering the pulses of thy sane and equable heart,
Tuning a verse for thee.

O Earth, that hast no voice, confide to me a voice!
O harvest of my lands! O boundless summer growths!
O lavish, brown, parturient earth! O infinite, teeming womb!
A verse to seek, to see, to narrate thee.

3

Ever upon this stage,
Is acted God's calm, annual drama,
Gorgeous processions, songs of birds,
Sunrise, that fullest feeds and freshens most the soul,
The heaving sea, the waves upon the shore, the musical,
        strong waves,
The woods, the stalwart trees, the slender, tapering trees,
The flowers, the grass, the lilliput, countless
        armies of the grass,
The heat, the showers, the measureless pasturages,
The scenery of the snows, the winds' free orchestra,
The stretching, light-hung roof of clouds — the clear
        cerulean, and the bulging, silvery fringes,
The high dilating stars, the placid, beckoning stars,
The moving flocks and herds, the plains and emerald
        meadows,
The shows of all the varied lands, and all the growths
        and products.

4

Fecund America! To-day,
Thou art all over set in births and joys!
Thou groan'st with riches! thy wealth clothes thee as with a swathing garment!
Thou laughest loud with ache of great possessions!
A myriad-twining life, like interlacing vines, binds all thy vast demesne!
As some huge ship, freighted to water's edge, thou ridest
            into port!
As rain falls from the heaven, and vapors rise from earth,
            so have the precious values fallen
            upon thee, and risen out of thee!
Thou envy of the globe! thou miracle!
Thou, bathed, choked, swimming in plenty!
Thou lucky Mistress of the tranquil barns!
Thou Prairie Dame that sittest in the middle, and lookest
            out upon thy world. and lookest East,
            and lookest West!
Dispensatress, that by a word givest a thousand miles —
            that giv'st a million farms, and missest nothing!
Thou All-Acceptress — thou Hospitable —(thou only art
            hospitable, as God is hospitable.)

When late I sang, sad was my voice;
Sad were the shows around me, with deafening noise of hatred,
      and smoke of conflict;
In the midst of the armies, the Heroes, I stood,
Or pass'd with slow step through the wounded and dying.

But now I sing not War,
Nor the measur'd march of soldiers, nor the tents of camps,
Nor the regiments hastily coming up, deploying in line of battle.

No more the dead and wounded;
No more the sad, unnatural shows of War.

Ask'd room those flush'd immortal ranks? the first forth-stepping armies?
Ask room, alas, the ghastly ranks — the armies dread that follow'd.

6

(Pass-pass, ye proud brigades!
So handsome, dress'd in blue — with your tramping, sinewy legs;
With your shoulders young and strong — with your knapsacks and your muskets;
— How elate I stood and watch'd you, where, starting off, you march'd!

Pass; — then rattle, drums, again!
Scream, you steamers on the river, out of whistles loud and shrill,
      your salutes!
For an army heaves in sight — O another gathering army!
Swarming, trailing on the rear — O you dread, accruing army!
O you regiments so piteous, with your mortal diarrhoea! with your fever!
O my land's maimed darlings! with the plenteous bloody bandage
      and the crutch!
Lo! your pallid army follow'd!)

7

But on these days of brightness,
On the far-stretching beauteous landscape, the roads and lanes,
      the high-piled farm-wagons, and the fruits and barns,
Shall the dead intrude?

Ah, the dead to me mar not — they fit well in Nature;
They fit very well in the landscape, under the trees and grass,
And along the edge of the sky, in the horizon's far margin.

Nor do I forget you, departed;
Nor in winter or summer, my lost ones;
But most, in the open air, as now, when my soul is rapt and at
      peace — like pleasing phantoms,
Your dear memories, rising, glide silently by me.

8

I saw the day, the return of the Heroes;
(Yet the Heroes never surpass'd, shall never return;
Them, that day, I saw not.)

I saw the interminable Corps — I saw the processions of armies,
I saw them approaching, defiling by, with divisions,

Streaming northward, their work done, camping awhile in clusters of
        mighty camps.

No holiday soldiers! — youthful, yet veterans;
Worn, swart, handsome, strong, of the stock of homestead and workshop,
Harden'd of many a long campaign and sweaty march,
Inured on many a hard-fought, bloody field.

9

A pause — the armies wait;
A million flush'd, embattled conquerors wait;
The world, too, waits — then, soft as breaking night, and sure as dawn,
They melt — they disappear.

Exult, indeed, O lands! victorious lands!
Not there your victory, on those red, shuddering fields;
But here and hence your victory.

Melt, melt away, ye armies! disperse, ye blue-clad soldiers!
Resolve ye back again — give up, for good, your deadly arms;
Other the arms, the fields henceforth for you, or South or North,
 or East or West,
With saner wars — sweet wars — life-giving wars.

10

Loud, O my throat, and clear, O soul!
The season of thanks, and the voice of full-yielding;
The chant of joy and power for boundless fertility.

All till'd and untill'd fields expand before me;
I see the true arenas of my race — or first, or last,
Man's innocent and strong arenas.

I see the Heroes at other toils;
I see, well-wielded in their hands, the better weapons.

11

I see where America, Mother of All,
Well-pleased, with full-spanning eye, gazes forth, dwells long,
And counts the varied gathering of the products.

Busy the far, the sunlit panorama;
Prairie, orchard, and yellow grain of the North,
Cotton and rice of the South, and Louisianian cane;
Open, unseeded fallows, rich fields of clover and timothy,
Kine and horses feeding, and droves of sheep and swine,
And many a stately river flowing, and many a jocund brook,
And healthy uplands with their herby-perfumed breezes,
And the good green grass — that delicate miracle, the
         ever-recurring grass.

12

Toil on, Heroes! harvest the products!
Not alone on those warlike fields, the Mother of All,
With dilated form and lambent eyes, watch'd you.

Toil on, Heroes! Toil well! Handle the weapons well!
The Mother of All—yet here, as ever she watches you.

Well-pleased, America, thou beholdest,
Over the fields of the West, those crawling monsters,

The human-divine inventions, the labor-saving implements:
Beholdest, moving in every direction, imbued as with life, the
        revolving hay-rakes,
The steam-power reaping-machines, and the horse-power machines,
The engines, thrashers of grain, and cleaners of grain, well
        separating the straw — the nimble work of the patent pitch-fork;
Beholdest the newer saw-mill, the southern cotton-gin, and the rice-cleaner.

Beneath thy look, O Maternal,
With these, and else, and with their own strong hands, the Heroes harvest.

All gather, and all harvest;
(Yet but for thee, O Powerful! not a scythe might swing, as now in security;
Not a maize-stalk dangle, as now, its silken tassels in peace.)

Under thee only they harvest — even but a wisp of hay, under thy great face, only;
Harvest the wheat of Ohio, Illinois, Wisconsin — every barbed spear, under thee;
Harvest the maize of Missouri, Kentucky, Tennessee — each ear in its light-green sheath,
Gather the hay to its myriad mows, in the odorous, tranquil barns,
Oats to their bins — the white potato, the buckwheat of Michigan, to theirs;
Gather the cotton in Mississippi or Alabama — dig and hoard the golden,
       the sweet potato of Georgia and the Carolinas,
Clip the wool of California or Pennsylvania,
Cut the flax in the Middle States, or hemp, or tobacco in the Borders,
Pick the pea and the bean, or pull apples from the trees, or bunches of
       grapes from the vines,
Or aught that ripens in all These States, or North or South,
Under the beaming sun, and under Thee.

"Carol of Occupations"

Come closer to me;
Push close, my lovers, and take the best I possess;
Yield closer and closer, and give me the best you possess.

This is unfinish'd business with me — How is it with you?
(I was chill'd with the cold types, cylinder, wet paper between us.)

Male and Female!
I pass so poorly with paper and types, I must pass with the
        contact of bodies and souls.

American masses!
I do not thank you for liking me as I am, and liking the touch of me —
        I know that it is good for you to do so.

This is the carol of occupations;
In the labor of engines and trades, and the labor of fields, I
        find the developments,
And find the eternal meanings.

Workmen and Workwomen!
Were all educations, practical and ornamental, well display'd out of me,
        what would it amount to?
Were I as the head teacher, charitable proprietor, wise statesman, what
        would it amount to?
Were I to you as the boss employing and paying you, would that satisfy you?

The learn'd, virtuous, benevolent, and the usual terms;
A man like me, and never the usual terms.

Neither a servant or master am I;
I take no sooner a large price than a small price — I will have my own,
        whoever enjoys me;
I will be even with you, and you shall be even with me.
If you stand at work in a shop, I stand as nigh as the nighest in the
        same shop;
If you bestow gifts on your brother or dearest friend, I demand as good as
        your brother or dearest friend;
If your lover, husband, wife, is welcome by day or night, I must be
        personally as welcome;
If you become degraded, criminal, ill, then I become so for your sake;
If you remember your foolish and outlaw'd deeds, do you think I cannot
        remember my own foolish and outlaw'd deeds?

If you carouse at the table, I carouse at the opposite side
        of the table;
If you meet some stranger in the streets, and love him or her — why
        I often meet strangers in the street, and love them.

Why, what have you thought of yourself?
It is you then that thought yourself less?
Is it you that thought the President greater than you?
Or the rich better off than you? or the educated wiser than you?

Because you are greasy or pimpled, or that you were once drunk, or a thief,
Or diseas'd, or rheumatic, or a prostitute — or are so now;
Or from frivolity or impotence, or that you are no scholar,
        and never saw your name in print,
Do you give in that you are any less immortal?

Souls of men and women! it is not you I call unseen, unheard, untouchable
        and untouching;
It is not you I go argue pro and con about, and to settle whether you
        are alive or no;
I own publicly who you are, if nobody else owns.

Grown, half-grown, and babe, of this country and every country, in-doors and
        out-doors, one just as much as the other, I see,
And all else behind or through them.

The wife — and she is not one jot less than the husband;
The daughter — and she is just as good as the son;
The mother — and she is every bit as much as the father.

Offspring of ignorant and poor, boys apprenticed to trades,
Young fellows working on farms, and old fellows working on farms,
Sailor-men, merchant-men, coasters, immigrants,
All these I see — but nigher and farther the same I see;
None shall escape me, and none shall wish to escape me.

I bring what you much need, yet always have,
Not money, amours, dress, eating, but as good;
I send no agent or medium, offer no representative of value,
        but offer the value itself.

There is something that comes home to one now and perpetually;
It is not what is printed, preach'd, discussed — it eludes discussion
        and print;
It is not to be put in a book — it is not in this book;
It is for you, whoever you are — it is no farther from you than your hearing
        and sight are from you;

It is hinted by nearest, commonest, readiest — it is ever provoked by them.

You may read in many languages, yet read nothing about it;
You may read the President's Message, and read nothing about it there;
Nothing in the reports from the State department or Treasury department,
        or in the daily papers or the weekly papers,
Or in the census or revenue returns, prices current, or any accounts of stock.

The sun and stars that float in the open air;
The apple-shaped earth, and we upon it — surely the drift of them is
        something grand!
I do not know what it is, except that it is grand, and that it is happiness,
And that the enclosing purport of us here is not a speculation, or bon-mot,
        or reconnoissance,
And that it is not something which by luck may turn out well for us,
        and without luck must be a failure for us,
And not something which may yet be retracted in a certain contingency.

The light and shade, the curious sense of body and identity, the greed that
        with perfect complaisance devours all things, the endless pride and
        out-stretching of man, unspeakable joys and sorrows,
The wonder every one sees in every one else he sees, and the wonders that
        fill each minute of time forever,
What have you reckon'd them for, camerado?

Have you reckon'd them for a trade, or farm-work? or for the profits
        of a store?
Or to achieve yourself a position? or to fill a gentleman's leisure,
        or a lady's leisure?

Have you reckon'd the landscape took substance and form that it might be
        painted in a picture?
Or men and women that they might be written of, and songs sung?
Or the attraction of gravity, and the great laws and harmonious combinations,
        and the fluids of the air, as subjects for the savants?
Or the brown land and the blue sea for maps and charts?
Or the stars to be put in constellations and named fancy names?
Or that the growth of seeds is for agricultural tables, or agriculture itself?

Old institutions — these arts, libraries, legends, collections, and the
        practice handed along in manufactures — will we rate them so high?
Will we rate our cash and business high? — I have no objection;
I rate them as high as the highest — then a child born of a woman and man
        I rate beyond all rate.

We thought our Union grand, and our Constitution grand;
I do not say they are not grand and good, for they are;
I am this day just as much in love with them as you;
Then I am in love with you, and with all my fellows upon the earth.

We consider bibles and religions divine — I do not say they are not divine;
I say they have all grown out of you, and may grow out of you still;
It is not they who give the life — it is you who give the life;
Leaves are not more shed from the trees, or trees from the earth, than they
    are shed out of you.

When the psalm sings instead of the singer;
When the script preaches instead of the preacher;
When the pulpit descends and goes, instead of the carver that carved
    the supporting desk;
When I can touch the body of books, by night or by day, and when they touch
    my body back again;
When a university course convinces, like a slumbering woman and child
    convince;
When the minted gold in the vault smiles like the night-watchman's
    daughter;
When warrantee deeds loafe in chairs opposite, and are my friendly
    companions;
I intend to reach them my hand, and make as much of them as I do of men
    and women like you.

The sum of all known reverence I add up in you, whoever you are;
The President is there in the White House for you — it is not you who are
       here for him;
The Secretaries act in their bureaus for you — not you here for them;
The Congress convenes every Twelfth-month for you;
Laws, courts, the forming of States, the charter of cities, the
       going and coming of commerce and mails, are all for you.

List close, my scholars dear!
All doctrines, all politics and civilization, exurge from you;
All sculpture and monuments, and anything inscribed anywhere, are
       tallied in you;
The gist of histories and statistics as far back as the records reach,
       is in you this hour, and myths and tales the same;
If you were not breathing and walking here, where would they all be?
The most renown'd poems would be ashes, orations and plays would be vacuums.

All architecture is what you do to it when you look upon it;
(Did you think it was in the white or gray stone? or the lines of the
       arches and cornices?)

All music is what awakes from you when you are reminded by the instruments;
It is not the violins and the cornets — it is not the oboe nor the
       beating drums, nor the score of the baritone singer singing his sweet romanza —
       nor that of the men's chorus, nor that of the women's chorus,
It is nearer and farther than they.

Will the whole come back then?
Can each see signs of the best by a look in the looking glass? is there
       nothing greater or more?
Does all sit there with you, with the mystic, unseen Soul?

Strange and hard that paradox true I give;
Objects gross and the unseen Soul are one.

House-building, measuring, sawing the boards;
Blacksmithing, glass-blowing, nail-making, coopering, tin-roofing,
       shingle-dressing,
Ship-joining, dock-building, fish-curing, ferrying, flagging of
       side-walks by flaggers,
The pump, the pile-driver, the great derrick, the coal-kiln and brick-kiln,
Coal mines, and all that is down there, — the lamps in the darkness,
       echoes, songs, what meditations, what vast native thoughts looking
       through smutch'd faces,

Iron-works, forge-fires in the mountains, or by the river-banks —
       men around feeling the melt with huge crowbars — lumps of
       ore, the due combining of ore, limestone, coal — the blast-
       furnace and the puddling-furnace, the loup-lump at the bottom
       of the melt at last — the rolling mill, the stumpy bars of
       pig-iron, the strong, clean-shaped T-rail for railroads;
Oil-works, silk-works, white-lead-works, the sugar-house, steam-saws,
       the great mills and factories;
Stone-cutting, shapely trimmings for facades, or window or door-lintels —
       the mallet, the tooth-chisel, the jib to protect the thumb,
Oakum, the oakum-chisel, the caulking-iron — the kettle of boiling
       vault-cement, and the fire under the kettle,
The cotton-bale, the stevedore's hook, the saw and buck of the sawyer,
       the mould of the moulder, the working-knife of the butcher, the
       ice-saw, and all the work with ice,
The implements for daguerreotyping — the tools of the rigger, grappler,
       sail-maker, block-maker,
Goods of gutta-percha-papier-maché, colors, brushes, brush-making,
       glazier's implements,
The veneer and glue-pot, the confectioner's ornaments, the decanter
       and glasses, the shears and flat-iron,
The awl and knee-strap, the pint measure and quart measure, the counter
       and stool, the writing-pen of quill or metal — the making of
       all sorts of edged tools,
The brewery, brewing, the malt, the vats, every thing that is done by
       brewers, also by wine-makers, also vinegar-makers,
Leather-dressing, coach-making, boiler-making, rope-twisting,
       distilling, sign-painting, lime-burning, cotton-picking — electro-
       plating, electrotyping, stereotyping,
Stave-machines, planing-machines, reaping-machines, ploughing-machines,
       thrashing-machines, steam wagons,
The cart of the carman, the omnibus, the ponderous dray;
Pyrotechny, letting off color'd fire-works at night, fancy figures and jets;
Beef on the butcher's stall, the slaughter-house of the butcher, the butcher
       in his killing-clothes,
The pens of live pork, the killing-hammer, the hog-hook, the scalder's tub,
       gutting, the cutter's cleaver, the packer's maul, and the
       plenteous winter-work of pork-packing;
Flour-works, grinding of wheat, rye, maize, rice — the barrels and the
       half and quarter barrels, the loaded barges, the high piles
       on wharves and levees;
The men, and the work of men, on railroads, coasters, fish-boats, canals;

The daily routine of your own or any man's life — the shop, yard,
        store, or factory;
These shows all near you by day and night — workman! whoever you are,
        your daily life!
In that and them the heft of the heaviest — in them far more than you
        estimated, and far less also;
In them realities for you and me — in them poems for you and me;
In them, not yourself — you and your Soul enclose all things, regardless of
        estimation;
In them the development good — in them, all themes and hints.

I do not affirm what you see beyond is futile — I do not advise
        you to stop;
I do not say leadings you thought great are not great;
But I say that none lead to greater, than those lead to.

Will you seek afar off? you surely come back at last,
In things best known to you, finding the best, or as good as the best,
In folks nearest to you finding the sweetest, strongest, lovingest;
Happiness, knowledge, not in another place, but this place — not for
        another hour, but this hour;
Man in the first you see or touch — always in friend, brother, nighest
        neighbor — Woman in mother, lover, wife;
The popular tastes and employments taking precedence in poems or anywhere,
You workwomen and workmen of these States having your own divine
        and strong life,
And all else giving place to men and women like you.

Excerpts from "Crossing Brooklyn Ferry"

Others will enter the gates of the ferry, and cross from shore to shore;
Others will watch the run of the flood-tide;

Others will see the shipping of Manhattan north and west, and the
        heights of Brooklyn to the south and east;
Others will see the islands large and small;
Fifty years hence, others will see them as they cross, the sun half an hour high;
A hundred years hence, or ever so many hundred years hence, others will see them,
Will enjoy the sunset, the pouring in of the flood-tide, the falling back
        to the sea of the ebb-tide.

"An Old Man's Thought of School"

An old man's thought of School;
An old man, gathering youthful memories and blooms, that youth
        itself cannot.

Now only do I know you!
O fair auroral skies! O morning dew upon the grass!

And these I see — these sparkling eyes,
These stores of mystic meaning — these young lives,
Building, equipping, like a fleet of ships — immortal ships!
Soon to sail out over the measureless seas,
On the Soul's voyage.

Only a lot of boys and girls?
Only the tiresome spelling, writing, ciphering classes?
Only a Public School?

Ah more — infinitely more;
(As George Fox rais'd his warning cry, "Is it this pile of brick
        and mortar — these dead floors, windows, rails — you call the church?
Why this is not the church at all — the Church is living, ever living Souls.")

And you, America,
Cast you the real reckoning for your present?
The lights and shadows of your future — good or evil?
To girlhood, boyhood look — the Teacher and the School.

"There Was a Child Went Forth"

There was a child went forth every day;
And the first object he look'd upon, that object he became;
And that object became part of him for the day, or a certain part of
        the day, or for many years, or stretching cycles of years.

The early lilacs became part of this child,
And grass, and white and red morning-glories, and white and
        red clover, and the song of the phœbe-bird,
And the Third-month lambs, and the sow's pink-faint litter,
        and the mare's foal, and the cow's calf,
And the noisy brood of the barn-yard, or by the mire of the pond-side,
And the fish suspending themselves so curiously below there — and the
        beautiful curious liquid,
And the water-plants with their graceful flat heads — all became
        part of him.

The field-sprouts of Fourth-month and Fifth-month became part of him;
Winter-grain sprouts, and those of the light-yellow corn, and the
        esculent roots of the garden,
And the apple-trees cover'd with blossoms, and the fruit afterward,
        and wood-berries, and the commonest weeds by the road;
And the old drunkard staggering home from the out-house of the tavern,
        whence he had lately risen,
And the school-mistress that pass'd on her way to the school,
And the friendly boys that pass'd — and the quarrelsome boys,
And the tidy and fresh-cheek'd girls — and the barefoot negro boy and girl,
And all the changes of city and country, wherever he went.

His own parents,
He that father'd him, and she that had conceiv'd him in her womb,
          and birth'd him,
They gave this child more of themselves than that;
They gave him afterward every day — they became part of him.

The mother at home, quietly placing the dishes on the supper-table;
The mother with mild words — clean her cap and gown, a wholesome odor
       falling off her person and clothes as she walks by;
The father, strong, self-sufficient, manly, mean, anger'd, unjust;
The blow, the quick loud word, the tight bargain, the crafty lure,
The family usages, the language, the company, the furniture — the yearning and
       swelling heart,
Affection that will not be gainsay'd — the sense of what is real — the thought if,
       after all, it should prove unreal,
The doubts of day-time and the doubts of night-time — the curious whether and how,
Whether that which appears so is so, or is it all flashes and specks?
Men and women crowding fast in the streets — if they are not flashes and specks,
       what are they?
The streets themselves, and the facades of houses, and goods in the windows,
Vehicles, teams, the heavy-plank'd wharves — the huge crossing at the ferries,
The village on the highland, seen from afar at sunset — the river between,
Shadows, aureola and mist, the light falling on roofs and gables of white
       or brown, three miles off,
The schooner near by, sleepily dropping down the tide — the little boat
       slack-tow'd astern,
The hurrying tumbling waves, quick-broken crests, slapping,
The strata of color'd clouds, the long bar of maroon-tint, away
       solitary by itself — the spread of purity it lies motionless in,
The horizon's edge, the flying sea-crow, the fragrance of salt marsh
       and shore mud;
These became part of that child who went forth every day, and who
       now goes, and will always go forth every day.

"That Music Always Round Me"

That music always round me, unceasing, unbeginning —
      yet long untaught I did not hear;
But now the chorus I hear, and am elated;
A tenor, strong, ascending, with power and health,
      with glad notes of day-break I hear,
A soprano, at intervals, sailing buoyantly over
      the tops of immense waves,
A transparent bass, shuddering lusciously under
      and through the universe,
The triumphant tutti — the funeral wailings with
      sweet flutes and violins, — all these
      I fill myself with;
I hear not the volumes of sound merely — I am
      moved by the exquisite meanings,
I listen to the different voices winding in and out,
      striving, contending with fiery vehemence
      to excel each other in emotion;
I do not think the performers know themselves —
      but now I think I begin to know them.

"In Midnight Sleep"

In midnight sleep, of many a face of anguish,
Of the look at first of the mortally wounded — of
          that indescribable look;
Of the dead on their backs, with arms extended wide,
          I dream, I dream, I dream.

Of scenes of nature, fields and mountains;
Of skies, so beauteous after a storm — and at night
          the moon so unearthly bright,
Shining sweetly, shining down, where we dig the
          trenches and gather the heaps,
          I dream, I dream, I dream.

Long, long have they pass'd — faces and trenches
          and fields;
Where through the carnage I moved with a callous
          composure — or away from the fallen,
Onward I sped at the time — But now of their
          forms at night,
          I dream, I dream, I dream.

"It Is I Too, the Sleepless Widow"

It is I too, the sleepless widow, looking out on the winter midnight
I see the sparkles of starshine on the icy and pallid earth.

A shroud I see, and I am the shroud — I wrap a body and lie in the
       coffin,

It is dark here underground — it is not evil or pain here — it
       is blank here, for reasons.

It seems to me that everything in the light and air ought to be happy,
Whoever is not in his coffin and the dark grave, let him know
       he has enough.

"Good-bye My Fancy!"

Good-bye my fancy!
Farewell dear mate, dear love!
I'm going away, I know not where,
Or to what fortune, or whether I may ever see you again,
So Good-bye my Fancy.

Now for my last — let me look back a moment;
The slower fainter ticking of the clock is in me,
Exit, nightfall, and soon the heart-thud stopping.
Long have we lived, joy'd, caress'd together;
Delightful! — now separation — Good-bye my Fancy.

Yet let me not be too hasty,
Long indeed have we lived, slept, filter'd, become really blended into one;
Then if we die we die together, (yes, we'll remain one),
If we go anywhere we'll go together to meet what happens,
May-be we'll be better off and blither, and learn something,
May-be it is yourself now really ushering me to the true songs, (who knows?)
May-be it is you the mortal knob really undoing, turning — so now finally,
Good-bye — and hail! my Fancy.

"I Bequeath Myself to the Dirt"

I bequeath myself to the dirt to grow from the grass I love,
If you want me again look for me under your boot soles.

You will hardly know who I am or what I mean,
But I shall be good health to you nevertheless,
And filter and fibre your blood.

Failing to fetch me at first keep encouraged,
Missing me one place search another,
I stop somewhere waiting for you.

PHOTO CREDITS